YOUNG GEOGRAPHER

SETTLEMENTS

NICK MILLEA

Wayland

Young Geographer

The Changing Earth
Food and Farming
Journeys
Natural Resources
Protecting the Planet
Settlements
The World's Population
The World's Weather

Editor: Sarah Doughty
Designer: Mark Whitchurch
Consultant: Dr Tony Binns, geography lecturer at Sussex
University

Front cover picture: The skyline of Los Angeles, in California,
USA.
Back cover picture: An open air market in a village in Peru,
South America.
Frontispiece: Bergen in Norway is a major port and the country's
second largest city.

First published in 1992 by
Wayland (Publishers) Ltd
61 Western Road, Hove
East Sussex BN3 1JD, England

© Copyright 1992 Wayland (Publishers) Ltd

British Library Cataloguing in Publication Data
Millea, Nick
   Settlements. – (Young Geographer Series)
   I. Title. II. Series
   910.09173

ISBN 0 7502 0442 7

Typeset by Type Study, Scarborough, England
Printed in Italy by Rotolito Lombarda S.p.A
Bound in France by A.G.M.

National Curriculum Attainment Targets

This book is most directly relevant to the following
Attainment Targets in the Geography National Curriculum
at Key Stage 2. The information can help in the following
ways:

Attainment Target 2 (Knowledge and understanding of
places) Describing similarities and differences between the
local area and another locality; comparing features and
occupations of the local area with other localities; explaining
why some activities in the local area are located where they
are.

Attainment Target 4 (Human geography) Demonstrating an
understanding that most homes are part of a settlement and
that settlements vary in size; giving reasons why people
change their homes; identifying features of settlements
which reveal their origins and analyzing the factors that have
influenced the location and growth of individual settlements;
explaining why few people live in some areas and many in
others; describing the layout and function of a settlement;
giving reasons for growth of economic activities in particular
locations.

Contents

All the words that are in **bold** appear in the glossary on page 30.

Introduction

A settlement can be described as a grouping of people living in one **location**. Such groupings can be very small indeed, perhaps made up of no more than one or two homes situated in the countryside. Other groupings can be very large, stretching many kilometres and providing homes for huge numbers of people, such as in London or Mexico City.

As well as homes, these large settlements need other buildings to provide **services** for the people who live there. In larger settlements you can usually find schools, shops, offices, factories, hospitals, public transport and places of worship. Large settlements also usually have entertainment facilities like cinemas, leisure centres or parks.

All today's settlements developed from the same **origins**, whether they are **hamlets**, villages, towns, cities or **conurbations**. It is believed that the first settlements appeared about 4,000 years ago in part of the world which used to be called Mesopotamia (now known as Iran and Iraq), as well as China and India. These early settlements allowed people to live close together

Settlements can be very small and remote. This is a typical house in the Chilean mountains in South America.

Malaga in Spain is a modern city with a wide range of services.

to defend themselves, and to benefit from each other's skills. A settlement would normally grow up next to a river, providing people with a supply of water and drainage for nearby land to allow them to grow crops. The river would act as a transport route for trading goods with other settlements.

Settlements are now found in every country of the world, whether the country is a rich one like Germany or the USA, or a very poor one as can be seen in many parts of West Africa.

The ancient city of Moenjodaro in Pakistan is one of the world's oldest settlements.

The location of settlements

There are many reasons why a settlement should be located where it is. People in early times may have had very different reasons for choosing a place to settle than people would have today. For early settlers, an available supply of food and water might have been the most important reasons for choosing a **site**. The **local** soil, climate and fuel supply may have also been important considerations, too.

Khartoum, in Sudan, is located at the point where the Blue Nile and the White Nile meet.

Left This illustration from 1867 shows New York City's key location on Manhattan Island.

Below A modern view over Manhattan Island, showing how crowded New York City is today.

It is often possible to find out about a settlement's origin and how it grew. Settlements are often found at a crossing point of a river. Detroit in the USA for example, lies on a river between Lake Huron and Lake Erie. Other settlements grew up at a river's lowest bridging point. This is the nearest place to the sea where the river can be crossed. For example Khartoum in Sudan is located at the crossing point where two rivers meet.

A settlement may develop where a river forces a gap through hills. New York City has an ideal position at the Mohawk-Hudson Gap. From here there are routes north to Montreal in Canada, and west to the Great Lakes. Natural springs that

provide a water supply also attracted settlers. The town of San Hilario Sacalm in northern Spain grew because of its numerous springs. Settlements also developed around **spas** which were believed to cure sickness, such as at Bad Aussee in Austria. Ports attracted growth, and created the trading links that allow a settlement to develop.

The remote hilltop location of Machu Picchu in Peru kept the settlement safe from Spanish invaders in the sixteenth century.

Hilltops were often chosen as a location for a settlement because of their good defences. Machu Picchu in South America is situated high in the mountains of Peru for this reason. However a flat plain may also attract people because of the rich farmland it provides. Winnipeg in Canada for example is located on flat-lying land in the heart of the country's grain-producing prairie.

When **resources** such as valuable metals or fuel supplies are available in an area, a settlement will often grow up. If a valuable metal such as copper is discovered, people are required to work in the mines and these people will live in nearby settlements. When a resource is found in a **remote** location, then a new settlement will develop. Other settlements develop as markets, and often sell goods produced from settlements around it. Kashgar is a trading post in western China. Five major roads meet here and link together much of Central Asia.

More recent developments are **resorts**, where settlements are sited to attract holidaymakers. They are often by the sea such as on the Spanish 'costas'. Cheap air travel has made these resorts popular destinations for people from countries where the climate is cooler. Mountains also attract people keen on skiing – Les Deux Alpes in France has been developed purely as a holiday centre.

Finally, governments create new towns. The Netherlands for example, had become an over-crowded country where farmland was scarce. To ease the problem, Lelystad was designed as the main settlement of an area of **reclaimed land**, called Flevoland whose first settlers arrived in the 1970s.

Benidorm in Spain has grown rapidly to meet the needs of tourism.

How settlements grow

As settlements vary in size, different words are used to describe them. A settlement might be **rural** like a hamlet or village or **urban** like a town, city or conurbation, depending on its size and location. The number of people living in a settlement is known as its population. A hamlet may have only 20 people, while a conurbation like the greater Tokyo area is home for 12 million people. It is possible however, for a town to grow into a conurbation.

Settlements grow for a number of reasons. One of these may be political. People may be forced to move to another part of their own country or over the border to a neighbouring one. The town of Peshawar in Pakistan for example, expanded rapidly during the 1980s due to large numbers of people arriving to escape the war in neighbouring Afghanistan.

The effect of a government's politics can also be seen in the West Bank area of the Middle East.

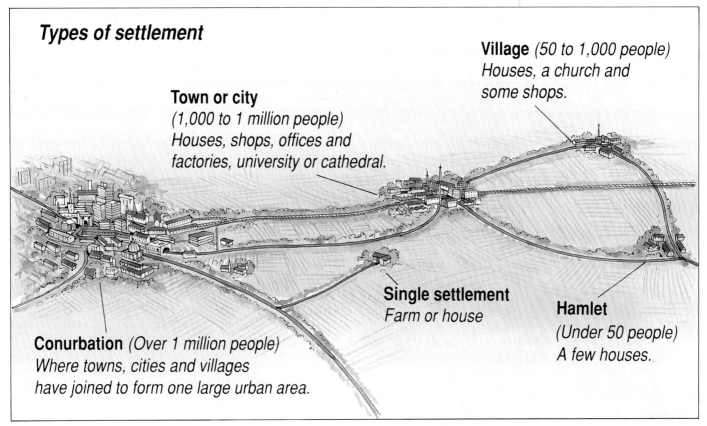

Types of settlement

Village (50 to 1,000 people)
Houses, a church and some shops.

Town or city
(1,000 to 1 million people)
Houses, shops, offices and factories, university or cathedral.

Single settlement
Farm or house

Hamlet
(Under 50 people)
A few houses.

Conurbation (Over 1 million people)
Where towns, cities and villages have joined to form one large urban area.

This illustration shows different sizes of settlements, from a single house to a conurbation.

Los Angeles, USA

Los Angeles was founded as a farming settlement in 1781 by just forty-four people. This is difficult to imagine as the greater Los Angeles area currently stretches 80 km west to east, with a population of over 13 million.

Above Freeways in Los Angeles, an area once covered by fruit trees.

Rapid growth began when the railway arrived in 1876 linking Los Angeles directly with the rest of the USA. Settlers were attracted to the west by cheap fares and a warm climate. Later developments include a port, industry and tourism.

Modern Los Angeles is now a vast city with a complex network of **freeways**. All the original farmland has been replaced by buildings.

Left Long Beach in Los Angeles in 1900. Tourism developed because of the area's favourable climate.

The West Bank has been Israeli land since it was captured in the war of 1967, and settlements have now increased in number and size to strengthen Israel's claim to this area.

The development of road and rail links help a settlement to grow.

Before the arrival of the railway in 1837, Crewe in north-west England was simply farmland. It then became the site of a major junction and engineering works, growing into a busy town. Forty years later Crewe had a population of 24,000 people.

Some settlements grow artificially. New towns are often planned by governments to attract people to an area normally used for farming, or not under **cultivation**. Nigeria for example has built a new capital at Abuja in the central part of the country. Lagos, the existing capital in the south-west, had become very **congested**, and is situated too far away from most of the Nigerian people.

Lagos in Nigeria has become overcrowded. Even these new roads have been unable to ease the congestion caused by large numbers of motor vehicles.

The Rhondda valley's population was at its peak in the early 1900s.

Rhondda Valley, South Wales

In 1801 the Rhondda valley of South Wales was isolated, and only 542 people lived there.

However, when large amounts of coal were discovered, many **collieries** opened including those at Treherbert in 1855. Railways were built to take coal to the docks and improve access to the valley.

By 1924 the settlement's population had risen to 170,000, but the coal mined in Rhondda quickly became less popular around the world. Ten years later half the workers had lost their jobs, so people started to leave the area.

By 1990 only 80,000 people lived in Rhondda. The collieries are being replaced by modern factories intended to bring the valley back to life.

Settlements can **decline** as well as grow. Resources such as coal can lead to the growth of a settlement, and support mining settlements like Katowice in Poland. But mining regions can also decline if the resource is either used up or is no longer required.

The layout of settlements

Settlements can sometimes be planned in advance, but they usually grow unplanned. There are two common types of settlement that develop. These are known as nucleated or dispersed. A nucleated village has all the buildings located together. Open farmland extends to the next village. When individual farms are located alone, the settlement pattern of the area is called dispersed.

A nucleated village is likely to have an old **nucleus**. A church, a village green or square, possibly some shops and a few houses. In Britain, housing tended to develop along roads leading out of the village, a feature known as ribbon development which was common in the 1930s. The 1970s and 1980s have seen newer housing added to the edges of villages, especially those closer to major towns.

Kettlewell in Britain is a nucleated settlement in the Yorkshire Dales.

Kano, Nigeria

Kano is a typical example of an unplanned Nigerian city. A 20 km-long wall surrounds the central area, only part of which is filled by buildings. A large market place and a palace lie at the heart of the city.

Most of Kano's buildings are crowded together in **compounds**, and each compound may be home for at least seven families. They are surrounded by high mud walls which rise above a network of alleyways. In 1984 access was improved. Many compounds were demolished to make room for roads, which have started to alter the original congested city layout.

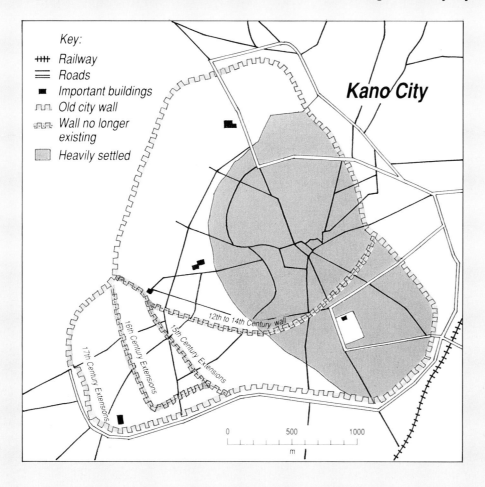

Key:
- ┼┼┼ Railway
- ≡ Roads
- ■ Important buildings
- ⏛ Old city wall
- ⏛ Wall no longer existing
- ▒ Heavily settled

Kano City

12th to 14th Century wall

16th Century Extensions

17th Century Extensions

15th Century Extensions

0   500   1000
m

Kano's old centre is located in the eastern walled area, where only Muslims can live. Further west, modern Kano has developed.

Buildings that make up an urban area tend to be organized into separate zones, resembling rings. Large shops and offices are found in the centre of town. This is called the **central business district** or CBD. The tallest buildings are found in this area because land is more expensive. Inner-city planners know that it is cheaper to build upwards than along costly ground.

The next zone will be filled with public buildings – the town hall, cathedral or perhaps a castle.

The layout of a settlement arranged in rings or zones (right) and its cross-section (below right).

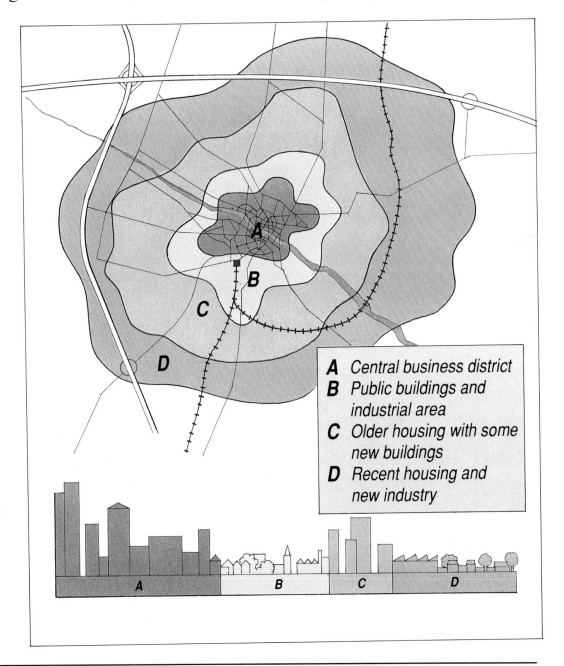

A Central business district
B Public buildings and industrial area
C Older housing with some new buildings
D Recent housing and new industry

Canberra, Australia

Canberra was founded in 1908, when it was chosen to be Australia's new capital city. The American architect Walter Burley Griffin won a competition to design a city, based on two circles separated by a lake.

Canberra was planned as a city of parks and gardens with Capital Hill and its government buildings lying to the south and City Hill to the north. Today only parts of the city conform to the designer's original plans.

Broad avenues spread outwards from the circles leading to housing areas with their shops and sports facilities. The road pattern looks like the spokes in wheels making it a very unusual layout for a city.

Right A map of Canberra. For a major city, Canberra has very little industrial development.

***Above** Canberra is a planned city of straight lines and plentiful greenery.*

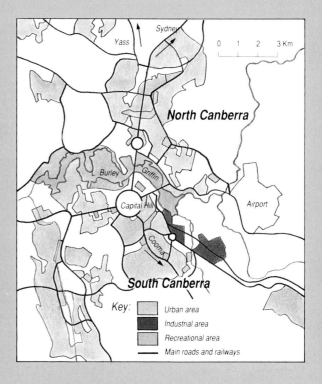

Old industrial buildings can be found here too, although many may no longer be in use. A third zone is made up of older housing, situated close to the factories of the second zone so people can travel to work easily. These houses are built very close together.

In the outer fourth ring we are likely to find more recent housing with large gardens or new industry at the edge of the built-up area. Locating in the outer zone gives industries both better road transport links and cheaper land **rents** than near the centre.

How settlements work

Settlements have at least one **function**. This is what a settlement does. The larger the settlement, the more functions it will have.

A capital city's major function is to act as a base for government, like Brussels, capital of Belgium and headquarters for the European Community. Ports have a number of different functions. A seaport like Kobe in Japan will deal with heavy goods, whilst Murmansk in Russia specializes as a naval dockyard and Bergen in Norway has fishing as its main function.

Some settlements act as religious, cultural or business centres. Mecca's prime function is that of Islam's principal religious centre, Florence in Italy thrives on its role as a

Mecca in Saudi Arabia is the principal centre for Muslims.

Hamburg, Germany

Hamburg is a major port. This is the River Elbe, busy with shipping traffic.

Hamburg is Germany's second largest city. It is also an international settlement with sixty ships a day arriving at the port and 140 airlines flying to the city. For those who live and work in Hamburg, there is also a tram and underground railway system to move people quickly around the urban area.

The city's functions include government, trade and newspapers. The major industries include chemicals, iron and steel, shipbuilding and food processing. There are also plenty of museums, theatres, art galleries, and cinemas as well as a zoo and a university.

cultural city, and Zurich in Switzerland is a centre of finance. Resources can also provide some settlements with their main function. For example, Kalgoorie in Western Australia is a remote gold mining town.

New towns have two common functions. They either provide homes for people from nearby crowded conurbations, or attract people to an area where they can find employment near to where they live.

Florence in Italy is famous for its museums and art galleries.

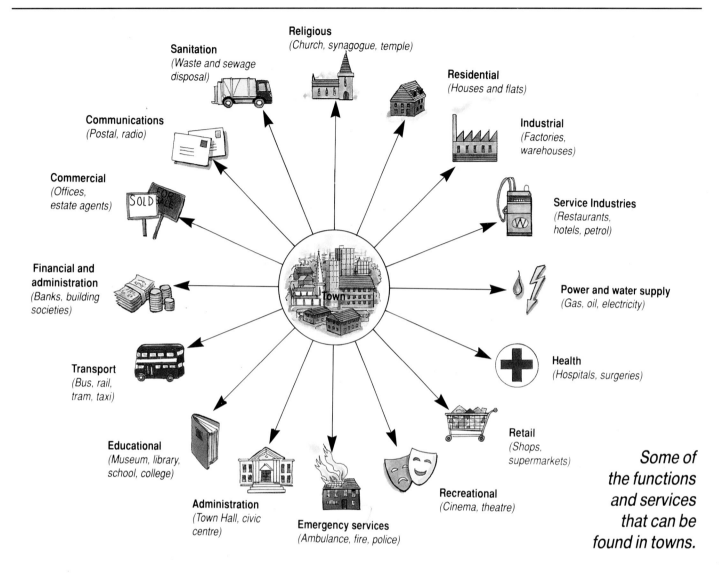

Religious
(Church, synagogue, temple)

Sanitation
(Waste and sewage disposal)

Residential
(Houses and flats)

Communications
(Postal, radio)

Industrial
(Factories, warehouses)

Commercial
(Offices, estate agents)

Service Industries
(Restaurants, hotels, petrol)

Financial and administration
(Banks, building societies)

Power and water supply
(Gas, oil, electricity)

Transport
(Bus, rail, tram, taxi)

Health
(Hospitals, surgeries)

Educational
(Museum, library, school, college)

Retail
(Shops, supermarkets)

Administration
(Town Hall, civic centre)

Recreational
(Cinema, theatre)

Emergency services
(Ambulance, fire, police)

Some of the functions and services that can be found in towns.

The number of services found in a settlement usually depends on its size. A major urban settlement will be used for shopping, entertainment and education. Offices, factories and various forms of public transport and communication services will also be found in an urban settlement. A town will also provide services such as water and a power supply to the people who live and work there. By contrast, a rural settlement will have very few functions. Sometimes they operate purely as a base for agriculture. Very few services are provided in rural settlements.

People in different settlements lead differing lifestyles. In a village that is remote from other settlements, the lives of the population may revolve entirely

Villagers in The Gambia winnowing groundnuts to separate them from the stalks.

Genieri, West Africa

Genieri is a small West African village in The Gambia. Life revolves around farming. The land is too salty to grow rice because of salt from the River Gambia, so the men grow groundnuts which they can sell, while the women grow crops in their gardens to feed the village. Another major function in Genieri is the grinding of grain to make flour which can take as long as five hours every day.

These activities are very important in a village with few functions where agriculture controls everyday life.

around the village. There may be no services like schools or hospitals and sometimes there are no roads. Compare this with a town you know where people use transport to travel to work, or make use of shops and enjoy the variety of entertainment on offer.

Problems of settlements

Throughout the world, settlements suffer from a wide range of problems, no matter what their size.

The location of a settlement may lead to its growth being restricted. Central Venice's site is restricted by its **lagoon** location. Built on a series of islands, there is nowhere for the city to expand. It cannot grow upwards because the land on which it stands is gradually sinking and larger buildings would only make the situation worse.

Cities can also **sprawl**. This usually occurs in larger cities of less developed countries. People arrive but cannot find a place to live so they choose to build their own houses around the edge of the city, so the city expands outwards.

People who live in a city may suffer from overcrowding and the effects of living too close to each other. São Paulo in Brazil is an example of a skyscraper city, where people live high above the ground. Many Eastern European cities also

The location of Venice restricts its growth outwards. The city is also slowly sinking into the ground.

A home in a shanty town in Lima. The house is built of a variety of materials.

Lima

Between 1940 and 1980, 2 million people moved to Lima from other parts of Peru in South America in search of work. However, Lima did not have enough houses for everybody, so people built their homes from whatever material they could find – bamboo, cardboard or tin.

Around one-third of Lima's population live in these shanty towns, known locally as 'young towns'. They occupy rural areas surrounding the city, either on hillsides or nestling in the flat desert. Houses are closely packed together without water or electricity, whilst poverty is widespread.

suffer the same problem with concrete tower blocks dominating an older city centre. Sometimes the quality of the housing is poor in a settlement, especially because of high-rise concrete apartments built in the 1960s.

People from urban settlements sometimes prefer to exchange their urban environment for a rural life. This has led to housing shortages in villages, where the local people can no longer find homes. Homelessness is another problem on a worldwide scale, especially in towns and cities.

Many Eastern European settlements have concrete high-rise housing.

Congestion is a problem that is common in our cities. In Europe many cities have historical centres with narrow streets. These become crowded with traffic, so **bypasses** have been created to ease the situation. In African cities such as Cairo or Lagos, the movement of traffic and goods is very difficult, but it may be too expensive to build new roads.

In cities where there are too many cars, another problem is created. In Athens, the **pollution** from cars is so bad that a yellow cloud has started to appear over the city. It is called nefos, or smog, caused by exhaust fumes. Cars have been banned from the centre of Athens on weekdays when pollution levels are very high. Other cities may soon need to take this sort of action, too.

Serious traffic congestion in Cairo, Egypt caused by cars, donkeys, buses and bicycles.

Right Despite wide roads and junctions controlled by traffic lights, congestion occurs in many US cities. Fumes pollute the air with poisonous gases.

Below Public transport in Hong Kong. Trams are one of the methods used to help people travel cheaply around the city.

In large cities it may be difficult for people to travel from one part of the city to another, so they need an efficient transport network. Hong Kong has tried to ease its situation with an expanding public transport network. There are ferries, buses an underground railway and taxis to carry the population around the city.

Changing settlements

Settlements are constantly changing. An increase in population will force the settlement to expand on to the surrounding land, perhaps taking over valuable agricultural country. Industry may choose to abandon sites towards city centres in favour of an out-of-town location. The central area will be left with a series of **derelict** buildings. These may be taken over and converted for leisure use as attempted with Baltimore's dockland area in the eastern USA which is now used for art galleries and shopping.

So the CBD of a town may be changing in its function as offices move out from the centre. If the CBD is congested, it slows down the movement of goods between urban settlements. New road networks develop surrounding the city and industry may move to a site on the edge of a city to gain **access** to a road. **Hypermarkets** are also attracted to such sites. Dieppe in France has its hypermarket located on the main road heading south from the town. There is usually plenty of car parking on the outside of towns unlike in the crowded centre. But outward movement may threaten the countryside beyond the town known as the **green belt**.

A hypermarket in France, built in an out-of-town location.

Shanghai, China

Shanghai is China's oldest city. It is suffering from an overcrowded central area which has grown too large for its current site. To improve Shanghai's housing, transport and pollution problems, in 1990 it was decided to develop an area called Pudong to reduce congestion in the city.

The Pudong area lies east of the centre across the Huangpu River. Pudong was once poor farmland, but industry and housing have gradually moved there.

Overcrowding in the city has encouraged the development of Pudong.

Now Shanghai expects two million people to eventually settle in Pudong. Other plans are for an underground railway, new mainline railway station and seaport, and a drinking water supply plant.

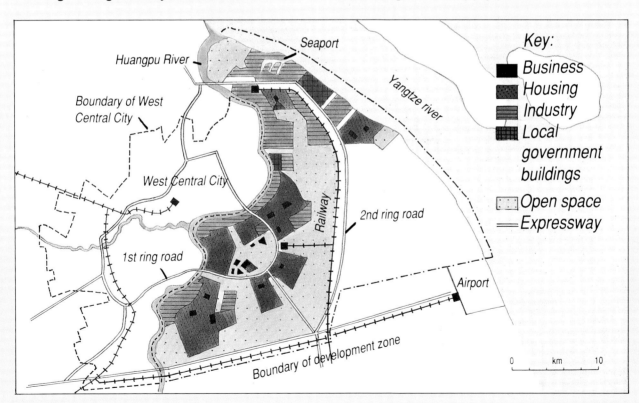

The plans for the development of Pudong, east of central Shanghai.

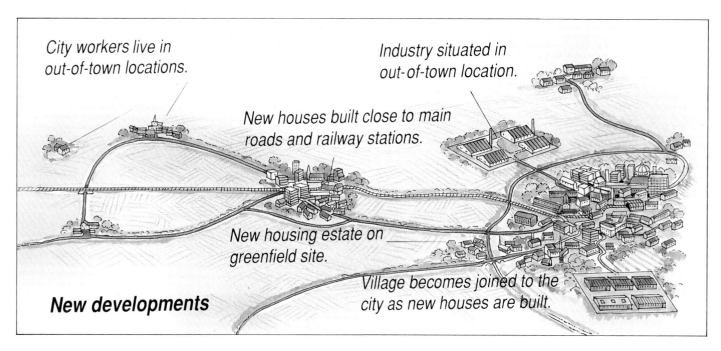

City workers live in out-of-town locations.

Industry situated in out-of-town location.

New houses built close to main roads and railway stations.

New housing estate on greenfield site.

New developments

Village becomes joined to the city as new houses are built.

This diagram shows how the pattern of settlements is changing.

Modern housing spreading into the countryside in western Britain.

Smaller settlements sometimes grow up around a city, separated from it by the countryside. These new towns are called satellite towns. They are usually carefully planned and provide houses and often jobs for people from the city. People no longer need to live near their workplace in a main city. Now with their own transport they can live further away, creating a change in rural settlement patterns. Because people want to move to villages in rural areas, new houses are often built on former farmland or woodland. So a village's function may become that of a **dormitory** settlement for a nearby city.

This modern bank is a sign of the change from farming to tourism.

Andorra-la-Vella, Pyrenees

With a population of 16,000, Andorra-la-Vella is one of Europe's smallest capitals. Situated in the Pyrenees, Andorra existed as a country traditionally based on farming and shepherding. Tourism developed in the 1950s once a road link to neighbouring France and Spain was completed.

Many farmers and shepherds became shopkeepers and hotel owners, allowing the small town to grow. Andorra is famous for selling normally expensive goods cheaply, so tourists can spend their money on Swiss watches, Japanese electronic goods, clothing and wine. This encourages further growth so the area near the town's main road is steadily developing into a large shopping centre.

Glossary

Access   A route such as a road or railway that allows people or goods to reach a destination.

Bypass   A road going round a settlement rather than through it.

Central business district   The central area of an urban settlement, sometimes called the CBD.

Colliery   A coal-mine.

Compounds   Enclosures in which local people are housed.

Congested   Overcrowded with traffic.

Conurbation   A number of formerly separate towns and cities now joined together.

Cultivation   Growing crops from the land.

Decline   To become smaller or lesser.

Derelict   Abandoned, and needing further development.

Dormitory   A settlement where housing is the main function.

Freeway   A major highway found in the USA.

Function   Goods or service provided by a settlement.

Green belt   Area of land at the edge of a settlement where new building is restricted.

Hamlet   A small village or group of houses.

Hypermarket   A huge shopping centre, usually on the edge of a town.

Lagoon   An area of water cut off from the sea.

Local   Restricted to a nearby area.

Location   Where a settlement is situated.

Nucleus   The central point of a settlement.

Origin   How a settlement begins.

Pollution   Damage to the environment caused by waste materials such as fumes from vehicles.

Reclaimed land   An area that used to be part of the sea and has now been converted into land.

Remote   Far away from where most people or towns are situated.

Rents   Payment for the use of land or building.

Resorts   Places where many people go for recreation.

Resources   Important materials that can be utilized, such as fuel or metals.

Rural   Belonging to the countryside rather than the city.

Services   Useful amenities supplied to people such as gas, oil or electricity.

Site   The exact place where something, such as a settlement, is situated.

Spas   Mineral springs.

Sprawl   When a city grows unevenly outwards from its edge.

Urban   Belonging to a town, city or conurbation.

Books to read

Bolwell, L. & Lines, C. *Towns and Cities* series (Wayland, 1985)

Bolwell, L. & Lines, C. *Where People Live* (Wayland, 1984)

Ferguson, S. *Village and Town Life* (Batsford, 1983)

Hernandez, X. & Comes, P. *A Town through History* (Wayland 1990)

Massey, J. & M. *The Urban Environment* (Franklin Watts, 1991)

Pollard, M. *Cities of the World* (Macmillan, 1987)

Notes for activities

Take a look at your own settlement on a map. See if the map gives you any ideas about how the settlement originated. Look for rivers, hills or transport routes for clues.

Travel to the centre of your nearest town. Starting from the centre, journey outwards and try to identify the settlement's various zones from the CBD to the outer ring.

Study a map of the closest rural area to your school. Look for settlements and try and decide if there is a nucleated, dispersed or other pattern. Try to explain the reasons for the pattern you discovered.

Using an atlas, find as many settlements as you can with populations larger than five million people.

Read a daily newspaper and see if you can find any examples of settlements with problems. Note where in the world the problems are occuring and try to find out what is being done to make improvements.

Think back over the past two or three years. Have there been any changes in your own settlement? Try and identify them. If not, think of ways in which the settlement may develop in the next two or three years.

Compare your own settlement to Genieri and Hamburg. Make a checklist of services – Cinema, Factory, Farming, Hospital, Market, Port, School, Shopping, Underground Railway and Zoo. Tick the services that are likely to occur in each settlement.

Index

Picture acknowledgements

The publishers would like to thank the following for allowing their photographs to be reproduced in this book: John Cornwell 13; Eye Ubiquitous 9 (David Cumming), 19 bottom and 22 (Derek Redfearn), 25 bottom (Helene Rogers), 28 bottom (Chris Bland); the Fotomas Index 7 (top); the Hutchison Library 11 top (Bernard Regent); J. Allan Cash Ltd 12, 15 top, 21, 24, 26, 27 top, 29; Panos Pictures 23 top (Paul Harrison), bottom (J. Hartley); Tony Stone Worldwide *cover* (Ken Briggs), *back cover, title page* (Hideo Kurihara), 8 (Robin Smith), 14 (Colin Raw), 17 (Fritz Prenzel), 18 (Nabeel Turner), 19 top (Oliver Benn); Topham Picture Library 11 bottom; Tropix 6 (D. Davis); Wayland Picture Library 4, 5 bottom (Jimmy Holmes); Zefa Picture Library 5 top, 7 bottom, 25 top. Artwork is by Stephen Wheele.